Mr Bean in Town

ROWAN ATKINSON, RICHARD CURTIS,
ROBIN DRISCOLL and
ANDREW CLIFFORD

Level 2

Retold by John Escott
Series Editors: Andy Hopkins and Jocelyn Potter

T0345860

Pearson Education Limited
Edinburgh Gate, Harlow,
Essex CM20 2JE, England
and Associated Companies throughout the world.

ISBN: 978-1-4058-8167-8

First published by Penguin Books 2001
This edition first published 2008

12

Original copyright © Rowan Atkinson, Richard Curtis, Robin Driscoll, Andrew Clifford
Text copyright © Pearson Education Ltd 2008

The moral right of the author has been asserted

Typeset by Graphicraft Ltd, Hong Kong
Set in 11/14pt Bembo
Printed in China
SWTC/12

Published by Pearson Education Ltd

Every effort has been made to trace the copyright holders and we apologise in advance
for any unintentional omissions. We would be pleased to insert the appropriate
acknowledgement in any subsequent edition of this publication.

For a complete list of the titles available in the Pearson English Readers series, please
visit www.pearsonenglishreaders.com. Alternatively, write to your local Pearson Education
office or to Pearson English Readers Marketing Department, Pearson Education,
Edinburgh Gate, Harlow, Essex CM20 2JE, England.

Contents

Introduction

*The meat was in Mr Bean's mouth, but he didn't want to **eat** it. He wanted to put it somewhere. But where? He looked at the man with the violin. He moved quickly. He pulled open the back of the man's trousers and opened his mouth. The meat fell inside the trousers!*

What happens when Mr Bean goes to a restaurant for his birthday dinner? He doesn't understand everything on the menu, and he doesn't like his food. He doesn't want to eat it, but what can he do? He tries to hide the food – in the strangest places!

The next day, he takes his clothes to the launderette. Oh dear, life is often difficult for Mr Bean! What happens in the launderette? He loses his trousers, of course!

The first *Mr Bean* story was on British television on 1 January 1990. There were fourteen half-hour stories about Mr Bean over the next five years. The last story, *Goodnight, Mr Bean*, was on television on 31 October 1995. Everybody liked this strange, funny little man with his little yellow car, and people in more than two hundred countries watched his stories on television. Rowan Atkinson was one of the writers, and he *is* Mr Bean. You can also see Mr Bean at the cinema or on video in the films *Bean* (1997) and *Mr Bean's Holiday* (2007).

The writers of these two very funny stories about the famous Mr Bean are Rowan Atkinson, Richard Curtis, Robin Driscoll and Andrew Clifford. Richard Curtis also wrote the famous films *Four Weddings and a Funeral* (1994), *Notting Hill* (1999) and *Love Actually* (2003).

Steak Tartare

It was Mr Bean's birthday, and he wanted to enjoy it! What could he do?

'How can I make this important day a *happy* day?' he thought. 'I know. I'll go out to a restaurant for dinner this evening! I'll enjoy that.'

Mr Bean didn't often eat in restaurants. They were sometimes very expensive. And he sometimes did things wrong when he was in a new or strange place.

Oh dear! Life wasn't easy for Mr Bean!

♦

That evening, Mr Bean put on a clean shirt. He put on his best coat and trousers. He put on his best shoes. Then he drove to a restaurant in the centre of town.

He arrived at eight o'clock and went inside. It was a very *nice* restaurant. Everybody was wearing their best clothes, and there were flowers on every table.

'I'm going to like it here,' thought Mr Bean. 'This is a good restaurant for my birthday dinner.'

The manager met him at the door.

'Good evening, sir,' he said. 'How are you? Would you like a table for one?'

'Yes, please,' said Mr Bean.

'Follow me, sir,' said the manager.

He walked across the room to a table, and Mr Bean went after him.

'Here you are, sir,' said the manager. 'This is a nice table.'

He pulled the chair away from the table. Then he waited for Mr Bean to sit down. Mr Bean looked at him.

1

'Why is he taking my chair away?' thought Mr Bean. 'What's he doing?'

And he pulled the chair away from the manager and sat down quickly.

When the manager went away, Mr Bean sat quietly for a minute. Then he remembered something. He took a birthday card and an envelope out of his jacket. Next, he took out a pen and wrote 'Happy Birthday, Bean' inside the card. Then he put the card into the envelope and wrote his name on the outside of it. He put it on the table, and put his pen back into his jacket.

After a minute or two, Mr Bean pretended to see the card for the first time.

'Oh! A card – for me?' he said.

He opened the envelope and took out the card. He read it carefully.

'Now that's nice!' he said. 'Somebody remembered my birthday!'

'Somebody remembered my birthday!'

2

And he stood the card on his table.

The manager arrived with the menu and gave it to Mr Bean. Mr Bean started to read it.

'Oh, dear!' he thought. 'Everything's very expensive! What can I have?'

Mr Bean got out his money. He had a ten-pound note and some coins. He put the money on to a plate.

'How much have I got?' he said, and he moved the money round on the plate. 'Ten, eleven . . . And forty, fifty, fifty-five! Eleven pounds and fifty-five pence.'

He looked at the menu again. What could he eat for eleven pounds fifty-five?

The manager came to his table.

'Are you ready, sir?' he asked.

'Yes,' said Mr Bean. He put his finger on the menu. 'I'll have that, please.'

The manager looked at the menu. 'The steak tartare, sir. Yes, of course.'

'Yes,' said Mr Bean. 'Steak.'

The manager took the menu and went away.

Mr Bean sat and looked round the restaurant. There were a lot of people in the room. There was a man and a woman at the next table. They ate and talked.

Suddenly, a waiter arrived at Mr Bean's table with a bottle of wine.

'Would you like to try the wine, sir?' he said.

'Oh, yes please,' said Mr Bean.

The waiter put some wine in Mr Bean's glass and Mr Bean had a drink. It was very nice! He smiled, and the waiter tried to put more wine into the glass.

Of course, the waiter was right. First, the customer tries his wine. When he is happy with it, the waiter gives him more wine. But Mr Bean didn't know this, and he quickly put his hand across the glass.

'Would you like to try the wine, sir?'

'No, thank you,' he said. 'I don't drink wine when I'm driving.'

The waiter looked at him strangely – and walked away. He *didn't* say, 'Why did you try the wine when you didn't want it, you stupid man!'

Mr Bean took the knife from the table and started to play with it. He pretended to be a bad man. He pretended to push the knife into somebody. But he didn't *really* want to kill anybody, of course. It was a game.

The woman at the next table looked at him angrily, and Mr Bean quickly moved the knife. Next, he hit the glasses and plate on his table with it. *Ping, ping, ping* they went! And after a minute, he played the song 'Happy Birthday' on the glasses. He smiled and thought, 'I'm very clever!'

But the woman at the next table didn't think, 'That's clever!'

or 'Oh yes, that's funny!' She thought, 'That man's really stupid!' And she looked hard at Mr Bean.

Mr Bean put the knife down and looked at his napkin.

'It's a very nice napkin,' he thought.

The waiter saw Mr Bean looking at his napkin. He didn't say anything, but suddenly – *flick!* – he opened it for Mr Bean.

'That's clever,' thought Mr Bean. 'I'll try that!'

And he began to move his napkin. *Flick! Flick! Flick!*

Suddenly, the napkin flew out of his hand. It flew across on to the next table. The woman at the table looked round again. But Mr Bean pretended not to see her. His face said, 'It's not *my* napkin!'

A minute later, the waiter arrived with his food. There was a large cover on the plate and Mr Bean couldn't see the food. But he gave the waiter the money on the table.

He began to move his napkin.

Customers don't *usually* give a waiter money when he arrives with the food. But the waiter didn't say anything. He took the money and put it in his jacket.

Mr Bean was happy. 'I'm doing everything right,' he thought.

The waiter took the cover off the plate and walked away. Mr Bean looked at the food in front of him. He put his nose near the meat and smelled it. Then he put his ear next to it.

'What's this?' he thought.

He put some of the meat into his mouth.

Suddenly, the manager arrived at his table.

'Is everything all right, sir?' he asked. 'Are you happy with everything?'

'Mmmmm,' said Mr Bean. He smiled.

The manager smiled, too. He walked away – and Mr Bean's face changed. There was no smile now. 'Aaagh!' he thought. 'They didn't cook this meat!'

But he had to eat it. 'I don't want people to think that I'm stupid,' he thought. 'But I'll never ask for steak tartare again! Never!'

He pushed his plate away.

But then the waiter went past his table.

'Is everything all right, sir?' he asked.

'Oh, yes,' said Mr Bean. He smiled. 'Yes, everything's very nice, thank you.'

He smiled and pretended to eat some meat. But the waiter went away before Mr Bean put it into his mouth.

'What can I do with it?' he thought. 'I can't eat this. Where can I hide it?'

Then he had an idea. Carefully, he put the meat into the mustard pot and put the cover on it.

'Where can I put some now?' he thought. 'I can't eat it, so I've got to hide all of it. Oh, yes, the flowers!'

He took the flowers out of the vase. But then the manager went past, so Mr Bean pretended to smell the flowers.

'Everything's very nice, thank you.'

'Mmm, very nice!' he said.

The manager smiled and walked away.

Quickly, Mr Bean put some meat into the vase and pushed the flowers in on top of it.

He looked round the table.

'Where next?' he thought. 'Yes! The bread!'

He took his knife and cut the bread roll. Then he quickly ate the middle of it. Now he could push some meat inside the roll. He did this, then he put the roll down.

He looked at the meat on his plate. 'There's a lot of it,' he thought. 'Where can I hide it now?'

He looked at the small plate on the table. Perhaps he could hide some meat under the plate. He looked round.

'Nobody's watching me,' he thought.

So he took more meat from the big plate in front of him,

Now he could push some meat inside the roll.

and put it under the small plate. Then he pushed down hard with his hand.

The waiter walked past his table again. Mr Bean smiled at him and put his arm on the plate. After the waiter went away, he pushed down on the small plate again.

'That's better,' he thought. 'Now you can't see the meat. Good. But there's more meat. Where can I hide it?'

He looked round the table.

'The sugar pot!' he thought. 'But it's got sugar in it. What can I do?'

He thought quickly, then he put some sugar into a wine glass. Next, he put some of the meat into the sugar pot. Then he put the sugar from the wine glass on top of it.

'Good!' he thought. 'Nobody can see it in there.'

Suddenly, Mr Bean could hear music.

'Where's that coming from?' he thought.

He looked round – and saw a man with a violin. After a minute or two, the man came across to Mr Bean's table and played for him.

Mr Bean smiled. 'This is nice,' he thought.

Then the man saw Mr Bean's birthday card, and the music changed. The man started to play 'Happy Birthday'!

The people at the other tables looked round when they heard the song. 'Who's having a birthday?' they thought. Then they saw Mr Bean and smiled at him. Mr Bean smiled back at them.

He pretended to eat some of the meat, but he didn't put it into his mouth. The man with the violin walked round Mr Bean's table and watched him. He played his violin and waited for Mr Bean to eat the meat. And he waited . . . and waited . . . and waited . . .

He waited . . . and waited . . . and waited . . .

'I'll have to eat some,' thought Mr Bean. 'He'll only go away when I eat it.'

So he put the meat into his mouth.

And the man with the violin turned away to the next table.

The meat was in Mr Bean's mouth, but he didn't want to *eat* it. He wanted to put it somewhere. But where? He looked at the man with the violin. He moved quickly. He pulled open the back of the man's trousers and opened his mouth. The meat fell inside the trousers!

He smiled. 'That was clever,' he thought.

The man with the violin moved round the next table. He played a song to the man and the woman. The music was very beautiful. They listened and drank their wine. They watched the man with the violin, so their eyes weren't on Mr Bean. *Nobody's* eyes were on Mr Bean. He saw this, and he had an idea.

Mr Bean quickly took the woman's bag from the floor. He opened it and pushed some meat inside it. Then he put the bag on the floor again.

But when he did this, he accidentally put his foot out.

The waiter walked past with some plates of food – and he fell over Mr Bean's foot! The plates fell on to Mr Bean's table, and on to the floor. There was a loud *CRASH!*, and the people at the other tables looked up quickly.

'What happened?' they said. Then they saw the waiter on the floor. 'Oh, dear!' they said.

Now Mr Bean had another idea. Here was the answer to his problem!

He moved very quickly. He pushed the meat from his plate on to the table with the other food. Then he pretended to be very angry.

'Look, you stupid man!' he said to the waiter. 'Oh, look at this!'

The waiter got up from the floor.

'I'm sorry, sir,' he said. 'I'm really *very* sorry.'

The manager arrived at the table.

'I'm very sorry, too, sir,' he said. 'Oh, the food –!'

'Yes, it's everywhere!' said Mr Bean. 'Look! It's in the mustard pot. It's in the bread roll. It's in the vase of flowers.' He took the woman's bag from the floor. 'And it's in here!' He pulled open the back of the violin player's trousers. 'And *here*!'

The waiter couldn't understand it.

'Go back to the kitchen,' the manager told him, and the waiter went away. Then the manager turned to Mr Bean. 'Please, sir,' he said. 'Come with me.'

'What?' said Mr Bean. 'Oh, yes, all right.'

The manager took Mr Bean to a clean table.

'Sit here, sir,' he said.

Mr Bean sat down.

'It's everywhere!' said Mr Bean. 'Look!'

'Thank you,' he said.

The manager opened Mr Bean's napkin. Then he got the birthday card from the other table. He put it on Mr Bean's clean table.

'Thank you,' said Mr Bean.

The man with the violin came across and played 'Happy Birthday' to him again. Mr Bean smiled. Now everything was all right.

'Now I can start again,' he thought. 'And this time I'll do everything right.'

The waiter arrived at Mr Bean's table. He put a plate in front of Mr Bean. The manager smiled and took off the cover.

Mr Bean looked down.

And he stopped smiling.

There, in front of him, was a very large plate – of steak tartare!

There, in front of him, was a very large plate – of steak tartare!

The Launderette

A lot of Mr Bean's clothes were dirty.

'I'll go to the launderette this morning,' he thought. 'I'll take the car.'

He put his dirty clothes into a very large black bag, and took the bag out to his car. He put it inside. Then he got in and drove to the launderette.

The launderette wasn't very busy that morning. Before Mr Bean arrived, there were only two women there. The younger woman was with the launderette manager.

'I've got to wash a lot of clothes,' the young woman said to the manager. 'I'll want a big washing machine.'

'This is one of our bigger machines,' said the manager. 'Use this.'

At that minute, Mr Bean arrived. He had the black bag on his back, and he couldn't get it through the launderette door.

'Oh!' he said.

He pulled and he pushed. He pushed and he pulled. In the end, he got the bag inside. He took it across to one of the washing machines.

'Money,' he thought. 'I want two one-pound coins for the washing machine.'

He took two one-pound coins out of his jacket and put them on the top of the machine.

But then Mr Bean saw a note above the washing machine: *Machines now cost £3.*

'Oh, no!' thought Mr Bean. 'Have I got another one-pound coin?'

He looked in his jacket and his trousers, but he could only find a five-pence coin. He put this on top of the washing machine.

Then Mr Bean remembered something. He *did* have another one-pound coin, but . . .

He looked round.

He started to pull out some string.

The young woman was next to the big washing machine. Mr Bean saw her putting some clothes into it. The launderette manager was busy in his little office.

'Nobody's watching me,' thought Mr Bean. 'Good.'

He opened the front of his trousers. Then he started to pull out some string.

The young woman turned suddenly and saw Mr Bean pulling the string out of his trousers.

'What *is* that man doing?' she thought.

Mr Bean saw her looking and turned away quickly.

But now the older woman looked at him. Her eyes opened wide. 'That's a strange man,' the woman thought. 'He's got *string* inside his trousers!'

On the end of the string was some paper, and inside the paper was a one-pound coin. Mr Bean smiled. He took the coin out of the paper and put it on the top of the washing machine. Then he put the five-pence coin back into his jacket.

Next, he opened the washing machine.

A man came into the launderette with a bag of dirty clothes under his arm. He was young and strong. When he saw Mr Bean, he smiled. But it wasn't a nice smile. He didn't say 'Hello' or 'Good morning'. He pushed Mr Bean away from the washing machine.

'What–!' began Mr Bean.

Then the young man pushed Mr Bean's one-pound coins on to the next machine.

Mr Bean was angry. He turned round to speak angrily – but then he saw the young man taking a white karate suit out of his bag.

'A karate suit!' thought Mr Bean. 'So he can fight. Perhaps I won't say anything.'

'A karate suit!'

The young man pushed his white karate suit into the washing machine. Then he put some money into the machine and sat down on a chair. He took a magazine out of his bag and began to read.

Mr Bean started to put his clothes into his washing machine. There were some pairs of underpants.

'Monday,' he said, and he put one pair into the machine. 'Tuesday.' He put the next pair into the machine. 'Thursday. Friday. Saturday.' Three pairs went into the machine.

Mr Bean stopped.

'Wednesday!' he thought. 'Where are Wednesday's underpants? Oh, it's Wednesday today, and I'm wearing them!'

What could he do? He had to wash them, so he had to take them off. He looked round.

'Where can I go?' he thought.

There was a partition near the washing machines.

'I'll go behind that,' he thought.

He started to walk to the partition, but the young man put his legs across the floor. He wanted to make Mr Bean angry. But Mr Bean remembered the karate suit. The man could fight! He walked round the young man's legs and said nothing.

He went behind the partition and carefully took off his brown trousers.

The young woman put some of her clothes into one of the very big washing machines. The other clothes were on the top of a smaller machine near the partition.

She didn't watch her clothes very carefully. She didn't see Mr Bean put a hand round the partition. And she didn't see him put his brown trousers down with her clothes.

Mr Bean took off his underpants – Wednesday's underpants. Then he put his hand round the partition. He took something – but it *wasn't* his brown trousers.

It was a long brown skirt.

It was a long brown skirt.

Mr Bean put on the skirt and came out from behind the partition. He walked back to his washing machine.

The young woman took the brown trousers from the top of the smaller washing machine. She didn't look at them. She put them into the big machine. Next, she shut the door of the machine and took a magazine. Then she sat down on a chair near the dryers and started to read. She had her back to Mr Bean, so she didn't see him wearing her skirt.

Mr Bean put his Wednesday underpants into his washing machine. Then he closed the door and put in his three one-pound coins.

He sat down on a chair – and saw the skirt!

'Oh, no!' he thought. 'What's this? A skirt? Where are my trousers?'

The young man walked past him, and Mr Bean tried to hide the skirt with his hands.

'I don't want him to see me in this skirt,' he thought. 'What will he think?'

The young man went across to a machine on the wall and bought a cup of conditioner.

Mr Bean got up and went back to the partition. He looked at the washing machine next to it and remembered the young woman's clothes.

'She put my trousers in the big washing machine with her things!' he thought.

He went across to the big washing machine and tried to open it. But he couldn't do it.

'I'll have to wait,' he thought, and he walked back to his chair.

The young man put his cup of conditioner on the top of his washing machine. Then he looked at Mr Bean – and saw the skirt. He started to laugh.

Mr Bean looked away quickly. He got his black bag – and a pair of underpants fell out of it.

'Oh! Sunday's underpants!' he said.

He tried to stop his washing machine and open the door. But the machine didn't stop.

'What can I do?' he thought. He looked down at the skirt. 'I know! I'll wear Sunday's underpants under this skirt! That's a good idea.'

He looked round, then went across to the conditioner machine, away from the other people. Carefully, he started to put on Sunday's underpants. He put his feet into them and – suddenly, he couldn't pull them up. He couldn't move them. There was a strange foot on them!

It was the young man's foot.

Mr Bean turned round and saw the young man laughing at

'What can I do?'

him. Mr Bean wanted to shout, 'Go away, you stupid man!' but he was too afraid.

After a minute, the young man laughed again and went back to his chair. Mr Bean quickly pulled up Sunday's underpants. He was angry.

'I don't like people laughing at me,' he thought, and he looked at the young man. 'What can I do to him? I can't fight him. He's too strong.'

Then he had an idea.

There was a coffee machine next to the machine for conditioner. Mr Bean went across to it and got a cup of black coffee. He smiled and walked back to his washing machine with the coffee.

Mr Bean carried the cup of conditioner to his chair.

The young man's eyes were on his magazine. He didn't look at Mr Bean or the washing machine.

'Now!' thought Mr Bean.

And he quickly changed the young man's cup of conditioner for his cup of black coffee. Then he carried the cup of conditioner to his chair and sat down.

He smiled. 'That will teach him a lesson,' he thought.

After a minute, the young man stood up and went to his machine. He had to put the conditioner into it now. He stood next to the machine and laughed at Mr Bean's skirt. So he didn't look at the cup when he put the 'conditioner' into the top of his washing machine.

But, of course, it wasn't conditioner. It was black coffee.

Mr Bean tried not to laugh.

The young man sat down in his chair again and looked across at his washing machine. There was a window in the door, and the young man could see his white karate suit going round and round in the water. But the suit wasn't white now. It was brown!

'What—!?' he shouted.

He jumped up. He ran across to the cup and looked inside it. Then he put it to his nose and smelled it.

'Coffee!' he shouted. Then he looked across at Mr Bean. 'Did you . . . ?'

Mr Bean didn't answer, but his face said, 'Who, me?' He pretended to drink his cup of 'coffee'. But it wasn't coffee, it was conditioner.

The young man went to find the launderette manager. Mr Bean stopped drinking and said, 'Aaaagh!'

♦

Mr Bean pretended to drink his cup of 'coffee'.

The young man showed the brown karate suit to the launderette manager.

'What's wrong, sir?' said the manager.

'This karate suit was white when I came in here,' said the young man. 'Now look at it!'

'What did you do to it?' said the manager.

'Me? I didn't do anything to it,' said the young man, angrily. He pulled the manager across to his washing machine. 'This is your machine. Is that right?'

'Y–yes,' said the manager.

The young man showed him the karate suit again.

'This cost me two hundred pounds!' he said. 'What are you going to do about it?'

'Er – will you come to my office please, sir?' said the manager. 'We can talk about it there.'

♦

Mr Bean sat opposite a large dryer. His underpants and other things were in the machine. They were clean now, and nearly dry.

Mr Bean waited.

After a minute, the dryer stopped. He got up and opened the door. Then he started to take out his clothes.

A minute or two later, the young woman came to the next dryer and started to take out her clothes. They were dry, too.

'Perhaps my trousers are in there!' thought Mr Bean.

The young woman took some clothes out of the machine and put them into a bag. Then she went back to the big washing machine for her other clothes.

Mr Bean moved quickly. He started to look through her clothes for his trousers, but he couldn't find them.

'Where are they?' he thought. 'They're here somewhere. Wait a minute! Perhaps she left them in the dryer.'

So he looked inside it. First, he put his head into the machine.

'Perhaps my trousers are in there!'

'I can't see anything,' he thought. 'It's too dark.'

Next, he climbed into the machine.

The young woman was busy at the big washing machine. She didn't see Mr Bean climb into the dryer. Then she took something out of the big washing machine. Her eyes opened wide.

'What's this?' she thought. 'A pair of *trousers*! I haven't got any brown trousers.'

She threw them on to one of the other washing machines, then she took her clothes across to the dryer.

Mr Bean was inside the dryer.

'Where are my trousers?' he thought.

Suddenly, the woman's washing began to fly into the machine – a skirt, a dress and some shirts.

'What–?' began Mr Bean.

Then the dryer door shut with a *BANG!*

'I can't get out!'

'Oh, no!' thought Mr Bean. He turned and climbed back to the door. 'Help!' he shouted through the window in the door. 'There's somebody in here!'

But the woman couldn't hear him. She took a pound coin and put it into the dryer.

Mr Bean hit the window in the dryer door. *Bang! Bang!* But nobody heard him.

'I can't get out!' he shouted.

Suddenly, it was very hot inside the dryer. There was a noise – and the machine started!

The clothes began to go round and round!

And Mr Bean began to go round and round...and round...and round...

ACTIVITIES

Steak Tartare   Pages 1–6

Before you read

1 Discuss these questions with another student.
   a What is your funniest story about a restaurant?
   b Which food do you like best? Which food don't you like?

2 Read the Introduction to the book and look at the pictures on pages 2, 4 and 5. What do you think of Mr Bean? Does he look: boring? funny? ugly? stupid? strange?

3 Look at the Word List at the back of the book. Which words can you use when you talk about:
   a food and restaurants?
   b clothes and washing?

While you read

4 What does Mr Bean do first in the restaurant? And then? Number the sentences 1–8.
   a He throws his napkin onto the next table.   .....
   b He opens a birthday card.   .....
   c He plays some music.   .....
   d He hides his food.   .....
   e He drinks some wine.   .....
   f He pulls a chair away from the manager.   .....
   g He listens to his food.   .....
   h He pays the waiter.   .....

After you read

5 What does Mr Bean pretend to do with these? Why?
   a a birthday card   c steak tartare
   b a knife

6 How do these people feel, and why?
   a Mr Bean, when he goes into the restaurant
   b Mr Bean, when the manager pulls the chair away from the table
   c Mr Bean, when he reads the menu

26

    d the waiter, after Mr Bean drinks some wine

    e the woman at the next table, about Mr Bean

    f Mr Bean, about his meat

7 Work with another student. Have this conversation between the woman and the man at the next table.

    Student A: You are the woman. You want to move to a different table. You think that Mr Bean is strange and stupid. Tell the man why.

    Student B: You are the man. You are happy at your table. You think that Mr Bean is funny and interesting. Tell the woman why.

Pages 7–12

Before you read

8 Discuss the pictures on pages 8, 9, 11 and 12. What is Mr Bean doing in these pictures? How does he feel? Why?

While you read

9 Are these sentences about Mr Bean right (✓) or wrong (✗)?

    a He hides his meat in the mustard pot and six other places.   .....

    b He puts sugar in his wine.   .....

    c He likes the violin music.   .....

    d The people in the restaurant sing 'Happy Birthday' to him.   .....

    e He eats his meat when the man with the violin watches him.   .....

    f He wants the waiter to fall over.   .....

    g The waiter knows that he is pretending to be angry.   .....

    h He is unhappy at the end of the story.   .....

After you read

10 Find the best words below and finish the sentences.

    a Mr Bean eats some of his bread roll because he

    b Mr Bean pushes down hard on a small plate because he

    c Mr Bean puts the sugar in his wine glass because he

d The other people in the restaurant smile because the man with the violin

e Mr Bean puts some meat in his mouth because he

f The woman at the next table doesn't see the meat in her bag because she

g Mr Bean puts his foot out because he

h The manager sends the waiter to the kitchen because Mr Bean

i Mr Bean stops smiling because he

1) plays 'Happy Birthday'.

2) is hiding some meat under it.

3) is putting the woman's bag on the floor.

4) has to eat more meat.

5) wants the man with the violin to go away.

6) is watching the man with the violin.

7) wants to hide some meat in the pot.

8) is angry.

9) wants to hide some meat in the middle of it.

11 Discuss these questions with another student. What do you think?

a Who do you feel most sorry for in this story? Why?

b How many accidents are there in this story? Which one is the funniest? Why?

c 'Mr Bean isn't a nice man.' Is he? Why (not)?

d Would you like Mr Bean to come to dinner at your house? Why (not)?

The Launderette   Pages 13–17

Before you read

12 Discuss these questions with another student.

a Do you go to launderettes? Why (not)?

b Look at the pictures on pages 14, 15 and 17. What is Mr Bean doing in these pictures? What problems is he going to have in this story?

13 <u>Underline</u> the right words.

    a Mr Bean finds a third one-pound coin in his *jacket / trousers*.

    b The young man wants to use Mr Bean's *money / washing machine*.

    c Mr Bean thinks that the young man is *strong / ugly*.

    d Mr Bean goes behind the partition because he wants to wash his *trousers / underpants*.

    e The young woman accidentally washes the *karate suit / trousers*.

    f Mr Bean accidentally *falls over the young man's legs / puts on a skirt*.

After you read

14 Who is thinking these words? Why?

    a 'Have I got another one-pound coin?'

    b 'Nobody's watching me. Good.'

    c 'What *is* that man doing?'

    d 'Perhaps I won't say anything.'

    e 'Thursday, Friday, Saturday.'

    f 'I'll go behind that.'

    g 'Oh, no! What's this?'

15 Work with another student. Have this telephone conversation between the young man in the launderette and a friend. (When you talk, don't look at the other student's face. Sit back to back.)

    Student A: You are the young man in the launderette. Telephone your friend and tell him / her about the strange man in the launderette. You don't like him and you want to start a fight with him. Tell your friend why.

    Student B: You are the young man's friend. Ask him questions. You think that your friend gets angry with people too quickly. You don't want him to start a fight. Tell him why.

Pages 18–24

Before you read

16 Look at the pictures on the next pages. Will Mr Bean:

    a get his trousers back?

    b have a fight with the young man?

    c have problems with the young woman?

    d be happy at the end of the story?

    Discuss your ideas with other students.

While you read

17 Are these sentences about Mr Bean (MB) or the young man (YM)?

    a He buys a cup of conditioner. .....

    b He tries to open the young woman's washing machine. .....

    c He puts his foot on a pair of underpants. .....

    d He puts coffee in a washing machine. .....

    e His clothes change colour. .....

    f He drinks some conditioner. .....

    g He is angry with the manager. .....

    h His trousers are in the big washing machine. .....

    i He climbs into a dryer. .....

After you read

18 Why does Mr Bean:

    a try to open the young woman's washing machine?

    b try to open his washing machine?

    c get angry with the young man?

    d smile when he gets a cup of coffee?

    e try not to laugh?

    f pretend to drink 'coffee'?

    g climb into the dryer?

    h shout for help?

19 Work with two other students. Have this conversation between the launderette manager, the young woman and the young man.

    Student A: You are the young woman. You are angry with the manager. You are unhappy about the launderette. Say why.

Student B: You are the young man. You are angry with the manager. You are unhappy about the launderette. Say why.

Student C: You are the manager. You think that the young man and woman made mistakes, not you. (You don't know about Mr Bean!) Tell them why.

Writing

20 You are the young woman at the next table in 'Steak Tartare'. You did not enjoy your evening in the restaurant and you want your money back. Write to the manager and tell him why.

21 You are the waiter in the restaurant. The manager thinks that you are a bad waiter. He thinks that you made a lot of mistakes when Mr Bean visited. You think that the manager is wrong about you. Write him a letter and tell him why.

22 You write for a food magazine. You were in the restaurant when Mr Bean visited. Write about the restaurant for your magazine. Is it a good restaurant? Why (not)? Write about it for your magazine.

23 You are Mr Bean. Did you enjoy your birthday? Why (not)? Write about it. Begin:
It was my birthday yesterday, so I went . . .

24 Write a funny short story about a visit to a restaurant when everything went wrong.

25 You are the young woman in 'The Launderette'. What happens next, when you take your clothes out of the dryer? Finish the story.

26 You are Mr Bean. You are not happy about your visit to the launderette. Write a letter to the manager about it. What is wrong with the launderette? How can the manager make it better?

27 You are Mr Bean's mother. You hear about your son in the restaurant and the launderette. You want your son to be more careful in future. Write to him about his mistakes. What can he do differently on his next visit to a restaurant and launderette?

WORD LIST *with example sentences*

bread roll (n) Do you want some butter with your *bread roll*?

coin (n) I'm driving into town. Have you got any *coins* for the car park?

conditioner (n) When I wash clothes, I always use *conditioner*.

cover (n) Put a *cover* over that meat before you put it away.

hide (v) You can't *hide* from me. I can see you under the table!

karate suit (n) Put on your *karate suit*! It's time for your class.

launderette (n) Is there a *launderette* near here? My clothes are all dirty.

machine (n) Put your dirty clothes in the *machine* and turn it on. The *washing machine* will start.

manager (n) The *manager* wants us to leave the shop.

mustard pot (n) Can you give me the *mustard pot*, please? I like mustard with meat.

napkin (n) She finished eating and then cleaned her hands with her *napkin*.

pair (n) Where are those shoes? You know – the blue *pair*.

partition (n) We have an open office, but there are *partitions* between the desks.

pretend (v + to + infinitive) They are not really animals, children – they *are pretending* to be animals!

smell (v) Can I *smell* chicken? I love chicken.

steak tartare (n) I don't think you cook *steak tartare*.

string (n) Put some *string* round the meat before you cook it.

underpants (n pl) He took off his trousers. His *underpants* were green and yellow!

vase (n) Put these flowers in the green *vase*, please.

violin (n) She plays the *violin* beautifully.